WINI TAYLOR

# Traveling on a Budget - Iceland

*A Guide to traveling the Ring Road in a Campervan*

# Contents

# Introduction

T raveling the world to see amazing places is just a pipe dream for some of us. We can't afford the airfare, hotels, cost of admission and currency exchanges! Before we know it, we're out thousands of dollars before stepping foot in the country.

I am curious minded, and an adventure seeking person. I love traveling to other countries, experiencing the local food, customs, and meeting the amazing people who call it home. I am not one for traveling to the "best" lists where every tourist goes. The lines are long, the price is higher, and the attraction is "Americanized" and designed to take my dollars.

If you love experiencing your destination like a local, enjoy meeting new people, and don't require 5 star everything, then this book is for you.

I'm writing this book to help those with a mindset for Adventure and with practical money discipline. A budget doesn't mean cheap, uncomfortable, or lacking. It means making decisions ahead of time and sticking to a plan.

Everyone knows about Iceland's dramatic natural beauty. From cascading waterfalls thundering down the mountain cliffs to the vibrant, colorful dancing auroras illuminating the Arctic sky. Icy fragmented glaciers flanked by black sand beaches and rugged lava rocks. During my trip I felt like I was on another planet.

Iceland is such an incredible, beautiful landscape, you're going to want to see as much of it as you can. It has become a popular destination, and it is also super expensive. You may choose to stay in hostels, Airbnb's, or camping to keep your costs down and save your precious money for some incredible day trips. Campervans are a popular way to see the country and you will have to book your van way in advance. I'll show you how to incorporate all three and recommend some great places to stay.

For this book I am going to focus on the infamous Ring Road. Iceland built the Ring Road to get all the tourists out of Reykjavik to see the rest of the country. Spreading the economic tourist wealth to the entire country and its citizens. The Ring Road is a 1322 km (820 miles) loop connecting most towns and villages in Iceland. It's a road trip renowned for its variety of scenery, passing many of Iceland's most iconic sites. A bucket list item you get to check.

Let's get started!

# Pre-Trip Planning

The first decision to make is When to go. Whether you want to see the Northern lights or see Iceland in warmer weather without Northern Lights. Or another way of asking is, how cold is too cold for you? Weather is a consideration during the peak months of the Northern lights. Because it is in the middle of winter, snow, road closures, and misery are a consideration. The best time to visit Iceland for the Northern lights is September to March.

The best time for summer-like weather, and outdoor activities is between June and August. However, Summer is the busiest time for tourists and pricing is more expensive during those peak months. Realistically, from April to October the weather is cold but not unbearable.

## Typical Weather in Reykjavik

- **June to August (peak time) - highs 12°C/54°F and lows 8°C/46°F**
- September to November (Fall) - highs 7°C/44°F and lows 4°C/39°F
- December to February (Winter) - highs 3°C/37°F and lows -2°C/28°F
- March to May (Spring) - highs 5°C/41°F and lows 0°C/32°F

I'm writing this book on December 17, 2023, and the 10-day forecast for North Iceland (Akureyi) shows highs around 20°F and lows in the teens.

Snow forecast of 2.8 in to 6.1 inches/day.

Whenever you decide to travel to Iceland, be sure to give yourself a week in the country not counting travel days. I recommend ten (10) total days, two travel days, and eight (8) for seeing the country. There is a lot to see and a lot of ground to cover, but it is worth the effort in planning. You can shorten this trip to seven (7) days by skipping a full day in the Westfjords and Snaefellsnes Peninsula or skipping a day on the east and west sides and continue along Route 1.

## Budget

Flights $700 – $1,000
 Transportation
 SUV $ 50 - $ 75/day
 Campervan $100 - $150/day
 Lodging $ 75 – $250/night
 Food $ 50 - $150/day
 Total $275 - $625/day - Plus your flight

A budget of $5,000 for 10 days is very realistic.

I visited in mid-March and the weather was cold but not miserable. Bundle up, be prepared, and you will be happy you went before the crowds arrive.

## Flights

Icelandair has direct flights from New York, Boston, Washington, D.C., Seattle, Denver, Minneapolis, and Orlando.

I'm in Florida and I checked direct flights from Orlando to Reykjavik and the average roundtrip flight is $800. Cheaper flights are available with stops in the Hub cities. My first trip to Iceland I flew the Redeye out of NY for $500.00. Search for deals, book early, and be willing to take the Redeye flight.You'll arrive in the morning and have the entire day to explore the south coast and Reykjavik.

## Transportation

Once you arrive you will want a vehicle. Since you will be driving to new locations each day and possibly taking in an evening under the Northern Lights, I recommend a Campervan. You could get an SUV and plan more nights at Hostels, or Airbnb. Both are easy to drive and easy to spend the night in if you need to. Rental cars, SUV or Van - $50 – 125/day.

This book will be focusing on a campervan, but you can just as easily rent a SUV and stay in guesthouses if your budget allows it. Even with a campervan you will want 1 or 2 nights in a Guesthouse or Hostel for some creature comforts.

## Lodging

Whether you choose a Campervan experience or not, you should know your rest stop and accommodation for each evening. Campervans are an extremely popular way to see Iceland, but inventory is limited so check on this early!

I recommend getting your campervan through Cozy Campers. Cozy Campers is a family run business and you can tell a lot of heart and soul went into the design of their campervan *and* their customer service. They have vans of different sizes, sleep 2 or 3. The 4x4 Cozy 3 XL serves as the perfect little home on wheels and a surprising beast for off-roading (and snowy) adventures.

If you decide to rent a SUV, can you say Hostels and Guesthouses? Because Iceland has become such a popular destination, you'll want to book as much in advance as possible. I highly recommend booking each night in advance. You can use Booking.com, Airbnb.com or search Hostels in Iceland. They are everywhere along Ring Road. Summer is the busiest time of year, so again, plan ahead. As for campgrounds, book those in advance too! Don't worry for now which campgrounds, I will give you ideas at each destination in the daily itinerary.

## What to Pack (Frugalicious)

### Food

Travel snacks and comfort food. I make my own meal bars (my recipe) and never, ever, travel without them. They are a good meal that I can count on to satisfy my hunger, keep me going, and not have stomach issues. I eat mine for breakfast and snacks. Whatever your comfort food is – bring it with you.Cliff bars, protein bars, jerky, trail mix, whatever you can pack in your luggage and bring enough for a week.

Coffee or Tea – bring your own instant, you can thank me later. I'm a coffee snob sometimes but I can drink just about any coffee, in any country. What I cannot do is – go without coffee. I bring my own. Again, comfort food. If you like instant food or MRE's (Meal, Ready-to Eat) bring a couple with you just in case. You will be traveling from destination to destination and the locations are remote and desolate. You may not see a store for miles and then when you do, depending on the time, it may not be open. We drove the South coast for a day trip which turned into "find a place to stay trip" and when we arrived, everything was closed. One hotel on a hill had a light on and we were lucky to get a room. The next morning, I was happy to have my meal bar and coffee in my bag.

In Reykjavik you can stock up on good travel food like oatmeal, jerky, ramen, Icelandic chocolate, Skyr, a few meats to grill and a hefty supply of snacks. The Campervan fridge can fit about 3 days of meals. By the time you need more food, you'll come across another grocery store like Kronan or Bonus along Ring Road.

## Clothing & Gear

Pack warm – long sleeves, long pants, sweaters, jacket/coat, scarves, wool skull cap, merino wool socks. *And pack **a rain jacket and rain pants** because you will want to keep the wet off you. There will be waterfalls, rain, wind, snow, and sea spray. I love Colombia gear but anything you prefer is fine. Shop on Amazon and find some deals. Just be sure you can fit your rain gear over your jacket, sweater, and pants. You will be layered up with clothing, so go bigger on the size. Waterproof, warm hiking boots and gloves are good travel companions too!

If you travel in the summer months, you will likely still need to pack for cold weather as their summer weather highs of 12°C/54°F and lows of 8°C/46°F

## Technology

Phone, laptop, back up battery and charger. European plug adaptor. Your plug won't work in the hotels, coffee shops, or anywhere else you may charge your devices. Invest in one or two plug adaptors. Phone and internet are available if your device is charged!

## Whale Watching

You can't go to Iceland without one excursion to see the whales. Abundant summer daylight combined with a unique mixture of cold and warm sea currents makes the Icelandic territorial waters home to a wide variety of krill and fish. As a result, Iceland is a bountiful feeding ground that attracts 24 different whale species, from the enormous sperm whale to the diminutive harbor porpoise.

The chances of spotting specific types of whales on a whale-watching trip vary depending on the port of departure. However, the minke whale is the most commonly sighted animal and can be seen all around Iceland throughout the year. Minke whales are the most common whales found in Iceland's waters, with many migrating here throughout summer and a few lingering through the winter months. They're small compared to other species but can still exceed 30 feet (9 meters) in length. Their behavior is usually rather shy, but due to their numbers, you can regularly see them from almost all whale-watching ports, including Reykjavik.

Whale watching tours for humpback whales operate out of Akureyri and Husavik in the north. The best time for humpback whales in the north is during summer months.

If you're eager to go orca watching in Iceland, they are most commonly seen in the East Fjords' rich herring grounds, along the South Coast, and around the Snaefellsnes Peninsula.

As you plan your trip keep in mind locations where you can see the whales.

# Northern Lights

If chasing the Northern Lights is a dream of yours, the best time to drive Iceland's Ring Road is between mid-September and early April. During these months, you'll have the best chance of clear, dark skies ideal for Aurora hunting. If you cannot handle hard winters, then try October or March.

The fall and winter months, from September to March, tend to be the prime time for the Northern Lights in Iceland. The long hours of darkness mean more opportunities to see the Aurora dancing overhead. And while winter brings colder temperatures, the solitude and snow-capped landscapes can make for a magical experience.

For the best views, head to spots away from city lights. Some of the top places along the Ring Road include:

- Jökulsárlón Glacier Lagoon - This stunning lagoon is a photographer's paradise and reflections of the Aurora in the still waters are unforgettable.
- Höfn - A charming fishing town with nearby glacier lakes perfect for Aurora viewing.
- Seyðisfjörður - A picturesque fjord town surrounded by mountains that block out light pollution.
- Mývatn - A geothermal area in northern Iceland with amazing landscapes, including volcanic craters and lava fields.
- Borgarfjörður Eystri - A secluded village in east Iceland with pristine nature all around.

To capture the Northern Lights on camera, use a tripod, point your lens north, and use a wide-angle lens with aperture of f/2.8 or lower and ISO of 800 to 3200. Take multiple long exposure shots (up to 30 seconds) and review/adjust as needed.

With the right timing, location, and photography tips, you'll be on your way to an epic Aurora adventure in Iceland. Chase your dreams and enjoy this natural wonder!

# Hiking

Every adventure to Iceland will undoubtedly include some hiking. The trailheads and "ideal hikes" are limitless.Hikes of varying distances and even the short walks along the Ring Road are exceptional. They are everywhere.The list is too long and overwhelming to list here. Every day included in the itinerary below will have hikes in each town, National Park, Lagoon, or coastline. A great resource for hiking along the Ring Road is The Big Outside. Here Michael Lanza outlines nine great hikes and they all line up with where you will be going along the Ring Road.

# Culture & Customs

Iceland is Nordic. Think Vikings, Norway, and Scandinavia. Public bathhouses are common, and Icelanders use them daily. And why wouldn't they? They have natural thermal waters which are piped into community pools and tubs. Wherever you go in Iceland there is water, water everywhere. Running hot down grassy hillsides, flowing clean and clear between tectonic plates, and frozen into glaciers. An abundance of volcano heated water in this landscape means you can sit outside and warm yourself through hot water.

## Hot pots & Community Pools

If you haven't heard of a hot pot, you're going to want to know all about them before visiting Iceland. Hot pots are tubs or bodies of water naturally heated by the earth. These dwellings are scattered all around Iceland and are accessible to anyone that can find them. Find a way to work these into your travels. Fortunately, there is an app for that! (App: Hot Pot Iceland) **Hot Pot Iceland** is an Iceland travel guide with locations of hot pots, swimming pools and **gas stations**. The app can be found on Google Play or Apple Store. For a small fee it will point you in the right direction. These are perfect getaways from your van and truly the epitome of relaxation. I have marked a couple of locations for **\*Hotpot** throughout the book.

**Language**

Despite having a small population of 360.000 people, Icelanders have their own language, which is, without doubt, a language that is most similar to the Viking Language or Old Norse. Due to confinement from complete isolation and hardly any outside influence, the language was kept pure and didn't change very much. In fact, Icelanders can still read the Icelandic Sagas, a literary treasure written in Old Norse dating back to the 13th and 14th centuries, without much difficulty.

## The Alphabet

**Aa Áá Bb Cc Dd Ðð Ee Éé Ff Gg Hh Ii Íí Jj Kk Ll Mm Nn Oo Óó Pp Qq Rr Ss Tt Uu Úú Vv Ww Xx Yy Ýý Þþ Ææ Zz Öö**

The Icelandic phonetics differs mostly in terms of a few vowels and some consonants. Some of the vowels, like A, E, I, O, U and Y have an identical vowel written with a comma on top. Contrary to what many think, the comma is not used as accentuation but signifies a different vowel sound. The specific letters of Ö and Æ can be found in some other Nordic language, but the phonetics of the latter is completely different.

As for the consonants, they are quite similar to the English language in pronunciation, except for a few letters like J which sounds like "y" in yoyo, R which is rolled similar to French and the special Icelandic characters of Þ and Ð mentioned before. What is also noticeable is that the consonants of C, Q, W and Z are not commonly used except for some loan words. The Icelandic tongue is a very phonetic language and when you learn how to pronounce some common words it gets easier. There are no silent letters, and the emphasis is always on the first syllable.

What does Icelandic sound like? Click the link for YouTube video on speaking Icelandic.

*Sun Voyager sculpture in Reykjavik*

# Iceland Geography and Regions

## How to See it All on The Ring Road

Iceland is packed full of natural wonders. From the coastline, to the volcanoes, to the glaciers, waterfalls, water boiling up from the earth, whales and the Auroras.

The areas to see are far and wide - Reykjavik, Golden Circle, South Coast, East Fjords, North Iceland, and West Fjords. This trip will take you around the country along Route 1, known as the Ring Road.

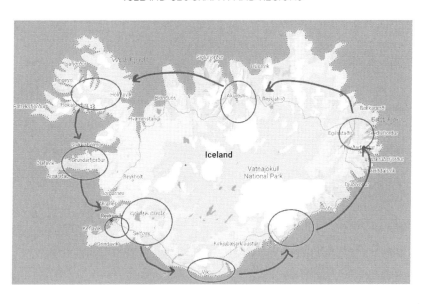

# Ring Road Itinerary

## Glaciers, Volcanoes, Waterfalls, Auroras, Thermal Waters, Whales & Birds

The focus of this book is the Ring Road. The Ring Road is Route 1 which circles the country. Afterall, you will be driving and "living" in a Campervan! Iceland's Ring Road offers spectacular landscapes, a sense of adventure, and a change of scenery about once an hour. You'll go from lush lagoons to moon-like craters, with dozens of epic waterfalls in between. Take detours to Fjords and other destinations off Route 1.

## Day 1 – Arrive in Reykjavik

**Pick up SUV or Campervan**. Relax at Blue Lagoon after a long flight and get settled in. Check Blue Lagoon's website for proper etiquette and what to expect.

If you want to skip the popularity of Blue Lagoon, try Hvammsvik Hot Springs. Just outside of Reykjavik, in the nearby fjord of Hvalfjordur, you will find Iceland's newest hot spring bathing spa. Hvammsvik Hot

Springs was opened in 2022, with the idea of incorporating the ebb and flow of the tides into the experience of bathing in warm geothermal water. The spa consists of eight natural hot spring pools of various sizes and temperatures, some of them being closer to the shoreline than others. Therefore, when the tide is high, the ocean flows into the geothermal pools that are nearest to the shore.

**Food** – Groceries and any provisions can be purchased in Reykjavik. Grocery stores Kronan and Bonus are popular and located along Ring Road. Fill the fridge and gas tank. Brace yourself for the cost. Your first trip to the grocery store will explain why I suggested bringing comfort food from home. Get local products whenever possible. Try their beer, their yogurt (Skyr), their fish, their meat. Produce is imported. As for water, Iceland offers some of the freshest water in the world. Don't pay for bottled water when you can just refill a large jug or two at the local gas station.

**Gas** – As you venture far from Reykjavík, it becomes much more desolate. It is not uncommon to drive for an hour or two at a time without passing through a single town along Ring Road. A good rule of thumb is to **never let our gas tank get below ½ tank**. You should be able to stick to this plan the entire trip. After long spans of nothing but extraordinary vistas, you will inevitably stumble upon a tiny town with at least one gas pump. When you stumble upon a gas pump don't be a penny pincher for the next one because there may not be another gas pump for miles. Many pumps are unmanned, and a **debit card** will be needed. I say debit card specifically, because Iceland gas stations require you to enter your entire a pin number and most credit cards do not have pin numbers.

If you do not want to spend your 1st night in Reykjavik and prefer a campsite outside of the main City, Hveragerði fits the bill. This area will lead you to the south coast with plenty of lighthouses and scenery. Hveragerði is a town and municipality in the south of Iceland, 45 km east of Reykjavík on Iceland's main Ring Road, Route 1. The river Varmá runs through the town. Hveragerði is the third smallest municipality in Iceland by size.

Camping available Reykjamörk Hveragerði Campsite *Hotpot* - Klambragil, Near Hveragerði. Klambragil is a hot river in an active geothermal field north of Hveragerði.

From Hveragerði you will have easy access to the Golden Circle on day 2 and be able to drive on to Seljalandsfoss or Vik after sightseeing.

You can also explore the south coast on Day 1 if you are up for it, via the lighthouse trail. The South Coast Lighthouse Trial takes you to PorlaksHöfn, Eyrarbakki, and Stokkseyri.

# Golden Circle and South Coast

## Day 2 – The Golden Circle

The infamous Golden Circle is a Must see – Geysir, Gullfoss, Strokker, Thingvellir. Enjoy the drive and stop at the various attractions which are all free. Depending on how much driving you enjoy, make your way to Selfoss, Seljalandsfoss, or Vik to stay the night. There are campgrounds outside of Selfoss in Stokkseyri if you do not want to drive on to Seljalandsfoss or Vik. There is Camping in Vik.

## Day 3 - Drive the South Coast to Jökulsárlón Lagoon

The southern part of Iceland is the flattest part of the country. The road follows the coastline. Stunning waterfalls, glacial scenery, and beautiful black sand beaches along the shorelines on the way to Jökulsárlón. As you head north up Route 1 to the Eastfjords, East Iceland and the many little villages and towns along the coast and nestled between mountains are some of the best locations to see the Northern Lights. **Aurora hotspot** Camping is available near Jökulsárlón Lagoon, and in Skaftafell.

# East Coast and East Fjords

## Day 4 - Jökulsárlón Glacier Lagoon, Vatnajökull National Park

J ökulsárlón is a glacial lagoon, bordering Vatnajökull National Park, and considered an **Aurora hotspot**. The blue waters are dotted with icebergs from the surrounding Breiðamerkurjökull Glacier, part of larger Vatnajökull Glacier. The Glacier Lagoon flows through a short waterway into the Atlantic Ocean, leaving chunks of ice on a black sand beach. In winter, the fish-filled lagoon hosts hundreds of seals.

All must see destinations. Vatnajökull National Park encompasses Skaftafell with magnificent views on the glacier, including the highest peak Hvannadalshnjukur. Finish up your day with a drive over to Höfn.

There are multiple guesthouses in Höfn, but only one campground. Camping Höfn. This tiny little fishing village is the lobster capital of Iceland.

## Day 5 – Eastfjords - From Höfn to the Egilsstaðir.

Höfn or Höfn í Hornafirði is an Icelandic fishing town in the southeastern part of the country. It lies near Hornafjörður fjord. The town, the second largest in the southeastern part of Iceland, offers scenic views of Vatnajökull.

The drive from Höfn to Egilsstaðir is a zigzag of fjords. During summer, it is possible to travel over the Öxi mountain pass on Route 939. This scenic gravel road shortens the way between Djúpivogur and Egilsstaðir by 68 km but requires extra precaution. A short drive from Egilsstaðir over to Seyðisfjörður on Route 93 for the Northern lights is worth the detour. **Aurora hotspot**

Many travelers mistake following only the main road through the East, bypassing the atmospheric Eastfjords with its wonderful slices of small-town Iceland.

A beautiful place to stay and get out of the van is Bragdavellir Cottages This place is perfect to stretch out, relax, enjoy endless hiking, horses, reindeer, nearby waterfalls, and the views. They are a 10 min drive from the town of Djúpivogur, where you can find a supermarket, coffee shop and restaurants.

**\*Hotpot**– On the way to Egilsstaðir take 953 to Mjoifjordur. Mjoifjordur roadside hotpot is in a staggeringly beautiful part of the Strandir region surrounded by mountains. To use the pool, you need to ask at the nearby farmhouse first. Mjóifjörður is a village of 7 people in East Iceland, sitting on a fjord of the same name. I think you can find the farmhouse to ask to use the pool.

# North Iceland and Akureyri

## Day 6 – From Egilsstaðir to Dettifoss and on to Akureyri

Day 6 is decision day on where to go next.depending on the weather and time of year you are traveling. Northern Iceland has huge mountain ranges to cross. Depending on what you want to fit in on your way to Akureyri. Dettifoss waterfall, Godafoss waterfall, Lake Mývatn, and Akureyri.

From Egilsstaðir, head to Dettifoss Waterfall and Lake Mývatn . Or skip Dettifoss and head to Lake Myvatn and onto Godafoss Waterfall before staying in Akureyi.

Leave Egilsstaðir and head to Dettifoss Waterfall and Akureyi. Taking route 1 to 864 will take you along the east side to Dettifoss, with views of Selfoss or take 862 on the west side. An easier drive with all the views. This is your choice as there are opinions from everyone as to which side is better. The terrain on 864 is rougher and may require 4x4. Either way – after Dettifoss get back to route 1 and on to Lake Myvatn or Akureyri for the night.

If driving the Ring Road from September to May, stay up to date on road conditions on Holtavörðuheiði, Öxnadalsheiði and Möðrudalsöræfum — these high mountain passes frequently close during storms or high winds.

Myvatn Nature Baths are the Blue Lagoon of Northern Iceland but on a smaller scale. Admission price $50. The car park has been extended and coach loads choke reception at times, but popularity comes for a reason, and it is charming, even if eggy smelly. It is also the closest you will get to swimming in a volcano around these parts.

**Lake Mývatn** is also considered an **Aurora hotspot**. Find a secluded spot along the shore of the lake to watch the Lights dance and flicker across the sky. The lake's calm, reflective surface doubles the beauty of the Aurora, while the surrounding lava fields provide a dramatic landscape. Fun fact – Myvatn loosely translated means "Mosquito Lake". At certain times in the summer, there are millions of small flies at the lake. The flies attract lots of birds to the area and are a vital source of food for the region. These swarms of flies are harmless, but annoying. If you are traveling to Myvatn in the summer, consider bringing a head net.

   **\*Hotpot** –Check out Hverfjall, Hverir, and Dimmuborgir.

**Akureyri** is a city at the base of Eyjafjörður Fjord in northern Iceland. The city center has the 1940 Akureyri Church. Nearby, the Akureyri Art Museum displays contemporary art from Iceland and farther afield. To the south are the Botanical Gardens, with specimens from across Iceland. Akureyi is a great place to restock your food before heading over to the Westfjords.

From Akureyri you can go on a Whale watching tour, hunt for Northern Lights, check out Laufas Turf houses or go horseback riding.

The Godafoss waterfall is spectacular. Located in northeastern Iceland. Godafoss, the "waterfall of the Gods," is one of Iceland's most iconic natural treasures. It can be easily accessed from Akureyri.

# Westfjords

## Day 7 – Westfjords

The Ring Road cuts off much of the western part of Iceland due to an inland route via Borgarfjörður, bypassing the wonders of the alpine Westfjords and Snæfellsnes Peninsula. But make no mistake: there is more to this region than its gas stations serving coffee and hot dogs. Roadside towns like Hvammstangi on your way to the Westfjords have plenty to see.

**The Westfjords are really only accessible in the summer months**, from May to September. Snowfall is heavy in the region, and the Westfjords sometimes get cut off from the rest of the country during winter. Due to its lower population, the roads are not regularly maintained as in the rest of the country. It's recommended to make use of the better road conditions in summer.

If you decide to make this trip in the winter months, you can carry on along Route 1 as there are plenty of villages and roadside towns to visit and hunt for Northern lights.

No matter the season, you should always **check the conditions of roads**

**in Iceland** before going on any trips and be prepared to adjust your plans if necessary. The local website for travel conditions https://www.road.is/travel-info/road-conditions-and-weather/

There are epic beaches tinted with mineral hues. There are great cliff faces teeming with sea birds. There are tiny fishing hamlets, mist-shrouded fjords, lonely headlands, and waterfalls that thunder with a sound and fury that stupefies. Geologically speaking, this is Iceland's most ancient corner: it's a place that feels mythic and mysterious, a land of lore straight out of the sagas.

Make your way to Dynjandi, Hornstrandir, pink-sands of Raudasandur, and the puffins at Latrabjarg.

The **Hornstrandir Nature Reserve** is one of the most isolated and untouched areas in Iceland, known for its dramatic landscapes and wildlife.

Being the least populated region of Iceland outside of the Highlands, the area has had an explosion in flora and fauna in the last decades, making it an excellent destination for those seeking out the best examples of Iceland's wildlife.

For bird watchers, Látrabjarg must feel close to Valhalla. Every summer, thousands upon thousands of seabirds flock to these 1,312-foot-high cliff faces (400m) to roost, soar, squabble, babble and breed. Even if birds aren't your thing, Látrabjarg is worth the journey: it's Iceland's most westerly point.

Þingeyraroddi is a newly opened campsite located in Þingeyri, one of the oldest towns in the Westfjords founded in 1787. The campsite is open all year round and has great facilities. There is a hot tub there, a playground for the kids, and even a volleyball court. However, it is at the most western tip of the Fjords. If you are planning on visiting the

Snaefellsnes Peninsula you should stay closer to Route 1 as the drive to the Peninsula may take 5 hours from Þingeyri.

# Final Days

## Day 8 - Snaefellsnes Peninsula

Depending on where you stay in Westfjords, day 9 can get long. Driving from Látrabjarg in the Westfjords to Snæfellsjökull may take 5 hours.

The Snæfellsnes Peninsula is a region in western Iceland known for its dramatic landscapes, often nicknamed "Iceland in Miniature" due to its wealth of diversity in the geography and scenery. At its western tip, Snæfellsjökull National Park is dominated by Snæfellsjökull Volcano, which is topped by a glacier. Nearby, a trail leads through lava fields to black-pebble Djúpalónssandur Beach. In Stykkishólmur fishing village, the 19th-century wood-frame Norwegian House is a regional museum with a craft shop.

The roadside towns of Borgarnesand, and Blönduós each have museums, pools, and restaurants well worth the stop.

## Day 9 – Back to Reykjavik

Leaving the Peninsula and making your way back to Reykjavik there is a short detour to see one more waterfall, Hraunfossar waterfall. The little detour is about 25 miles off Ring Road.From route 1 take 50 east toward Reykholt. Take 518 east to the waterfalls. This might be a bit out of the way if you make the journey over to the Snaefellsnes Peninsula.

Hraunfossar waterfalls are 40 km (25 miles) from the Ring Road.

Reykjavik has plenty to see and do. If you didn't take some time on Day 1 to see the city, Day 9 is the time to take in Reykjavik. The capital, and largest city in Iceland, Reykjavik sits on Faxaflói bay. There are many sculptures throughout the city, including the iconic Sun Voyager (Solfar). Multiple places to visit and see including the Harpa concert hall, the National Museum of Iceland, Hillgrimer's Church, the Settlement Exhibition. Cafés and shopping at Laugavegur. You can find you a local Pub for dinner and bathhouse to relax in before flying home.

## Day 10 – Fly Home

# Conclusion

I hope you enjoyed the book and planning your travels to Iceland. I just wanted to add an ending note regarding the itinerary. As you probably noticed there is a lot of flexibility in the places to go, see and do. Take your time and use google maps to estimate your travel time between destinations, and plot your own itinerary depending on your personal "must see" list. My itinerary encompasses just about everything in one way or another. Do you have to see "every" waterfall? Would you rather hunt the Northern lights? Are glaciers and hiking your thing? It's all up to you and ready for you to see.

I hope you have enjoyed reading this book as much as I have in writing it. One book cannot encompass everything there is to see and do, but in doing this research it has brought back all the vivid memories of my own journey to this remarkable country.

*Please take a moment to leave a favorable review if you have enjoyed the book. Your review will encourage others to adventure to Iceland and take the open road.

# Resources

*4x4 Camper Rental Iceland - 5-Star Campervans!* (2023, September 14). Cozy Campers. https://cozycampers.is/

*The Ring Road.* (n.d.). https://www.visiticeland.com/article/the-ring-road

*Friend in Iceland.* (2023, June 19). The Icelandic Language: Common Phrases & Vocabulary When Traveling In Iceland. Friend in Iceland. https://friend.is/the-icelandic-language/

Iceland, S. (n.d.). *Towns & regions.* Visit South Iceland. https://www.south.is/en/destinations/towns-regions/the-south-coast-lighthouse-trail

*Chasing the Northern Lights on Iceland's Ring Road: Ultimate guide.* (n.d.-b). Aurora Academy. https://www.auroracourses.eu/iceland-ring-road-aurora-guide#:

Lanza, M. (2023, October 22). 9 Great hikes and walks along Iceland's Ring Road - the big outside. *The Big Outside.* https://thebigoutside.com/9-great-hikes-and-walks-along-icelands-ring-road/

Tómas, A. (2023, August 30). *The ultimate guide to the Westfjords of Iceland.* Guide to Iceland. https://guidetoiceland.is/nature-info/the-wild-west fjords-of-iceland

Sverrisson, T. (2022, April 22). *Top 5 campsites in the Westfjords - Happy Campers.* Happy Campers. https://happycampers.is/top-5-campsites-in-the-westfjords/

*Road conditions and weather.* (n.d.). The Icelandic Road and Coastal Administration. https://www.road.is/travel-info/road-conditions-an d-weather/

Made in United States
North Haven, CT
14 June 2024

53619008R00026